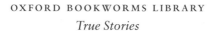

OXFORD BOOKWORMS LIBRARY

True Stories

The Boy-King
Tutankhamun

SCOTT LAUDER AND
WALTER MCGREGOR

Stage 1 (400 headwords)

Illustrated by Gavin Reece

Series Editor: Rachel Bladon
Founder Editors: Jennifer Bassett
and Tricia Hedge

OXFORD
UNIVERSITY PRESS

Great Clarendon Street, Oxford, OX2 6DP, United Kingdom

Oxford University Press is a department of the University of Oxford.
It furthers the University's objective of excellence in research, scholarship,
and education by publishing worldwide. Oxford is a registered trade
mark of Oxford University Press in the UK and in certain other countries

ISBN: 978 0 19 420932 8   Book
ISBN: 978 0 19 462059 8   Book and audio pack

Printed in China

Word count (main text): 5,227 words

For more information on the Oxford Bookworms Library,
visit www.oup.com/elt/gradedreaders

ACKNOWLEDGEMENTS

Cover image reproduced with permission from:
Bridgeman Images (Tutankhamun and his wife, Ankhesenamun, from his tomb,
New Kingdom, Egyptian 18th Dynasty/Valley of the Kings, Thebes, Egypt).

Illustrations by: Gavin Reece (story illustrations); Peter Bull (p.44).

Photographs reproduced with permission from: 123RF p.1 (Valley of Kings and the temple of
Hatchepsut/Matej Hudovernik); Getty Images pp.3 (Tutankhamun's funeral mask/
Robert Harding), 26 (Egyptian pyramids/Tobias Helbig), 39 (opening of
Tutankhamun's tomb/GraphicaArtis), 41 (Archaeologist Howard Carter
examining coffin of Tutankhamen/Time Life Pictures).

CONTENTS

PEOPLE IN THIS STORY

In Ancient Egypt

Aziru a boy from Amurru
the King of Amurru Aziru's father
Akhenaten Tutankhamun's father, a pharaoh of Egypt
Smenkhkare Akhenaten's oldest son
Tutankhaten (later **Tutankhamun**) Akhenaten's
   youngest son
Horemheb an important soldier
Ay vizier to the pharaohs
Sennedjem Tutankhamun and Aziru's teacher
Ankhesenamun Tutankhamun's wife

3,000 years later

Howard Carter an English Egyptologist
Lord Carnarvon a rich Englishman

MAP OF ANCIENT EGYPT

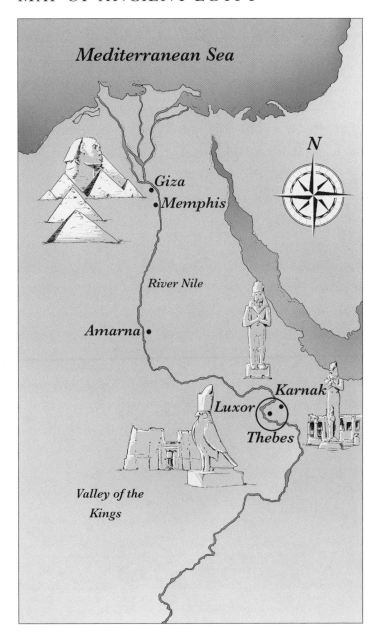

The Valley of the Kings in Egypt

The Valley of the Kings

In the hills near the old city of Thebes in Egypt, there is a valley. The Egyptians call it Wadi Al Muluk. In English, it is called the Valley of the Kings. The hills there are brown. There are no trees, and there is no water – only a blue sky, and a hot, hot sun. Today, many people come to this valley, most of them with cameras. But when the visitors leave and night comes, the valley is quiet – because this is the valley of the dead.

Long, long ago, Egyptians brought their dead pharaohs – their kings – to this valley. They made wonderful tombs for them, and put their bodies into beautiful coffins in the tombs. For five hundred years, the Egyptians did this; and there are sixty-three pharaohs, perhaps more, in the valley today. Many pharaohs were old when they died. But not all of them...

Three thousand years ago, men brought the dead body of Tutankhamun – the boy-king – into this valley. They put the body in a tomb, closed it, and went away. After some years, people forgot about the tomb, and soon, nobody remembered Tutankhamun's name.

Then, in 1922, an Englishman opened Tutankhamun's tomb, and found many wonderful things. Everyone wanted to see them, and suddenly the boy-king was famous. But we do not know a lot about him. Was he a good pharaoh?

Was he happy? Did he have many friends?

Perhaps in a different tomb, there are some papyri with stories about Tutankhamun. Perhaps a friend lived with Tutankhamun in the king's palace and knew him well. Perhaps the friend was a boy, and perhaps his name was Aziru...

Tutankhamun's mask

||
Aziru's Story Begins

My name is Aziru and I come from Amurru, a country to the north-east of Egypt. My father was king of Amurru.

One day, when I was young, my father called me to him. 'Aziru,' he said, 'who are the Hittites?'

'People from the north,' I answered. 'They don't like us or our friends, the Egyptians.'

My father looked at me. 'That's true,' he said quietly. 'But they are coming to Amurru. Because we are a small country, we can't stop them.'

I wanted to ask questions, but my father put up his hand. 'You must leave Amurru,' he said. 'You must go to Egypt and stay there. I know Pharaoh Akhenaten, and you can live with him, in the city of Amarna.'

Egypt! I could not speak! I did not know much about Egypt. Amurru was my home, and I did not want to leave my family and friends. I was afraid – but my father was the king, and I always listened to him.

'A boat is waiting for you,' said my father. 'You must go quickly.'

'Yes, Father,' I said.

So I left Amurru and went to Egypt. I was seven years old, and I never saw my father again.

I went by sea and by river, and after many, many days,

I arrived in Amarna. The city was very different from my home. My city was small, but in Amarna, there were hundreds of houses, and the streets were alive with thousands of people!

When I arrived at the palace in Amarna, soldiers took me to Pharaoh Akhenaten. The palace was beautiful, and much bigger than my father's.

The palace was beautiful, and much bigger than my father's.

I met Pharaoh Akhenaten, and he said: 'Aziru, you're like one of my sons now. Be happy here.'

I thanked him. Then I met Akhenaten's oldest son, Smenkhkare, and Akhenaten's youngest son, Tutankhaten. I smiled at Tutankhaten, but he looked away and said nothing.

So I began living in Akhenaten's beautiful palace. Slowly, I learned to speak like an Egyptian, dress like an Egyptian, and eat like an Egyptian.

I liked Egypt, but I did not have any friends. When I went to the palace gardens or to the river, nobody came with me. Tutankhaten did not speak to me. Why? Perhaps he did not like me because I was not Egyptian. I did not know.

I smiled at Tutankhaten, but he looked away.

III
A Talking Bird

A year after I arrived in Egypt, Pharaoh Akhenaten died; and after seventy days, the priests took his body to his tomb. Usually, pharaohs' tombs were in the Valley of the Kings or near Giza in the north of Egypt. But not Akhenaten's. His tomb was near Amarna.

Now Smenkhkare was the new pharaoh, the king of all Egypt. Out in the streets, the people of Amarna sang and played music. The Egyptians always sang when there was a new pharaoh, and this time I sang with them, too.

These were happy days, but I was not always happy in the palace. Smenkhkare was friendly to me, but Tutankhaten never spoke to me – and then there was Horemheb. Horemheb was the most important and powerful soldier in Egypt, and he did not like me. He was always angry, and I was afraid of him.

When Horemheb was in the palace, I often went to the palace gardens. I loved the gardens: there were lots of beautiful trees, animals, and birds. I liked the green parakeets the most. One of the parakeets always came and ate from my hand, and I called him Nefer. He could say one or two things, and I taught him some more. I talked to him a lot. I told him everything, and very often I told him about Horemheb.

One of the parakeets always came and ate from my hand.

One afternoon, I was in the garden with Nefer when somebody spoke behind me.

'What are you doing with that bird?'

I looked up and saw Tutankhaten's face.

'Answer me,' he said.

'I'm waiting,' I said. 'My parakeet usually talks to me, but today he's very quiet.'

Tutankhaten laughed. 'Birds can't talk,' he said.

'This one can.'

Tutankhaten had a bad leg, so he did not like to stand. He called for his chair, and sat down. The chair had gold on it, and its feet were like a lion's feet. Tutankhaten always asked for this chair because it was his father's old one, and Tutankhaten loved it.

He sat back in it now and looked at Nefer. 'Speak, bird!' he said.

We looked at Nefer and waited – but Nefer sat on my hand and said nothing.

After a minute or two, Tutankhaten laughed and stood up. 'I knew it. No bird can talk.'

Just then, Horemheb came into the garden. He walked across and stood next to us. 'Where's the pharaoh?' he asked angrily.

'I don't know,' answered Tutankhaten.

'I must find him,' said Horemheb, and he began to walk away when…

'Horemheb is angry!'

Horemheb looked at us, mouth open. 'Who said that?' he asked.

We did not answer.

'Horemheb is angry! Horemheb is angry!' Nefer called.

Horemheb's face went dark, and he looked at the little green bird. Then he looked at me. I began to say sorry, but he walked away.

When Horemheb was out of the gardens, Tutankhaten looked at me, and I smiled at him. Then we laughed. We could not stop laughing… and after that, I ate with Tutankhaten, laughed with him, and played with him.

Tutankhaten and I were now friends.

'Horemheb is angry!' Nefer called.

The New Pharaoh

When Tutankhaten was nine years old, his brother, the pharaoh Smenkhkare, died. Now Tutankhaten wore the crown of Egypt. On the crown, there was a snake, and the head of a big bird, the vulture. The snake was called the Uraeus, and it was important because only pharaohs wore the Uraeus. Egyptian pharaohs carried two sticks, too. These were called the crook and flail. The crook was the smallest of the two sticks, and when the people saw it, they remembered this: their pharaoh loved them very much. The flail was long, and when the people saw it, they remembered a different thing: their pharaoh was a good and powerful king.

Now Tutankhaten wore the crown of Egypt.

Because my friend was a very young pharaoh, many people helped him. Some of these people were powerful priests, but Tutankhaten listened most to Horemheb, the soldier, and to Ay, his vizier. All pharaohs had a vizier. The vizier was a very important man in the palace, and he helped the pharaoh very much.

Ay was from Tutankhaten's family. He was much older and much smaller than Horemheb, and he always spoke slowly and carefully. He smiled a lot, but his eyes were small and quick. Sometimes I thought, 'Are Ay and Horemheb true friends of Tutankhaten, or do they want to be pharaoh?'

The first years of Tutankhaten's time as pharaoh were not easy. There was a plague in Egypt, so many people were ill and many more died.

'Help us, Pharaoh!' they said. 'Stop the plague.'

But Tutankhaten could not. The plague killed and killed, and the people were angrier and angrier.

'Why are they angry with you?' I asked my friend Tutankhaten.

'Before my father was pharaoh, Egypt had lots of gods – Amun, Isis, Anubis, and many more,' he told me. 'But my father didn't like these gods. He said to the people, "Forget those old gods. We are going to have only one god – Aten, the Sun God." But now the people are saying, "Aten is not powerful. Aten cannot stop the plague – only our old god, Amun, can. He is the king of the gods. We must leave Amarna and go to Thebes! Thebes is Amun's city. He can help us there."'

'So are we going to move to Thebes?' I asked Tutankhaten.

'I don't know,' he said. 'Ay and Horemheb want to go, but the priests of Aten don't, and I must listen to them, too.'

We stayed in Amarna, but Tutankhaten changed his name to Tutankhamun. He did this because he wanted to please his people and Amun. But it did not help. More and more people died of the plague, and Egypt got angrier and angrier.

Two years went by. Often now, in the palace at Amarna, we could hear angry men in far-away rooms. It was Horemheb and Ay, and they were with Aten's priests. I did not understand much: I was only eleven years old. I was afraid, but Tutankhamun was not. He was never afraid.

After a time, things changed again.

'Now Ay and Horemheb look happy and Aten's priests look angry,' I said to Tutankhamun one evening. 'What's happening?'

There was some papyrus on the table in front of me, and I began making a picture.

'We're leaving Amarna,' said Tutankhamun, and he

sat down slowly. 'We're moving to Thebes.'

'Can I come with you?' I asked. 'I don't want to go home to Amurru.'

'Yes, of course! I can't leave my best friend.'

I smiled and finished my picture of two boys. When Tutankhamun saw it, he laughed.

'You're the pharaoh in this picture!' he said. 'You have the crook and flail in your hands and the crown on your head!'

'I know,' I answered. 'Now Horemheb can't be angry with me because I'm Pharaoh Aziru!'

I smiled and finished my picture of two boys.

Tutankhamun's leg hurt more every day, and he was only eleven years old, but now he stood up and spoke like a man. 'The old gods are important, and perhaps they're angry with us. But I'm going to make new temples for them, all across Egypt. We need to please the old gods, and the new temples can do that. Then the old gods can help Egypt, and Egypt can be rich again.'

'I want to see Thebes,' I said. 'I want to go on the Nile and…'

The door opened, and Horemheb walked into the room with Ay.

Horemheb looked at me, and I looked away.

'Horemheb and I are never going to be friends,' I thought. He always remembered that day with Nefer, my green parakeet.

'Everything is ready, my pharaoh,' said Ay quietly, and he smiled. 'We can leave tomorrow.'

'Good,' said Tutankhamun.

Horemheb said nothing, but his eyes stayed on me.

'Come, my pharaoh,' said Ay. 'You must sleep. We have a long day tomorrow and we must leave early.'

Tutankhamun smiled. 'A long day, perhaps. But more importantly, a *great* day.'

And it was true. After Tutankhamun left Amarna, he made many new temples for the old gods. The old gods were happy, and the Egyptian people were happy, too.

Tutankhamun made many new temples for the old gods.

A Lesson with Sennedjem

Every year, there was more and more gold in Egypt's new temples. Egypt was rich again, and the people loved their pharaoh. He gave them their old gods – gods like Amun, Isis, and Anubis – and the old gods smiled on Egypt.

Tutankhamun had a wife now, called Ankhesenamun. But he was only thirteen years old, and thirteen-year-old boys in palaces had teachers. Tutankhamun was like a brother to me, so when he had lessons, I had lessons, too. Our teacher was called Sennedjem, and we worked with him every day. I did not like listening to Sennedjem, and I did not like learning hieroglyphics, or hearing about the gods, or the stars. But Tutankhamun did.

One morning, I went to the Nile for a walk. Tutankhamun liked the river, but he did not often come with me now because his leg hurt more and more.

At the river, I walked slowly for some time and looked at the water and at the hills, red in the early morning sun. Then I heard a noise and looked down. At my feet, I saw a little brown frog. I liked frogs, so I put it in my pocket. Then I ran to the palace: I was late. I thought about Sennedjem's angry face and ran fast.

At my feet, I saw a little brown frog.

In the school room, I sat next to Tutankhamun, and Sennedjem began talking about Sothis. Sothis was an important star for the Egyptians. When Egyptians saw this star in the night sky, they were happy. They said: 'Soon the Nile is going to bring lots of water onto the fields – it's going to flood.'

The flood was very important in Egypt. Egyptians could grow many things when the waters of the Nile came onto the fields in the summer months.

Sennedjem talked and talked. And, of course, my eyes slowly began to close…

'Where does the water for the flood come from?' asked Tutankhamun.

'It comes from the gods. When the god Isis cries, this brings the water,' answered Sennedjem.

'Does the Nile flood every year?' asked Tutankhamun.

'No. Sometimes there is no flood, and… Aziru!' cried Sennedjem. 'Open your eyes!'

'Yes, teacher?' I said.

'Please write "Sothis",' said Sennedjem.

At that time, I was not good at hieroglyphics. I looked at Tutankhamun, and he smiled and put his head down.

'Did you hear me, Aziru?' said Sennedjem. 'Write "Sothis" in hieroglyphics. Now!'

'I… I…'

Tutankhamun laughed.

'I can't,' I said.

'I see,' said Sennedjem. 'And why not?'

'Because I don't have a reed,' I said. In Egypt, we took reeds from the river, and made them into pens with a knife.

Sennedjem looked at me angrily, then walked to his big table. He had his back to me, and suddenly, the frog in my pocket moved. I saw Sennedjem's cup of water on the table in front of me, and my hand went into my pocket…

Sennedjem came back with a reed. 'Now write "Sothis",' he said.

'Yes, teacher.'

Sennedjem watched me and took a big drink from his cup.

'What?' he cried. The cup fell from his hand, and water went all over the room. 'Who put a frog in my drink?'

'Who put a frog in my drink?'

Just then, Horemheb and Ay came in. 'What's the matter?' asked Ay.

'There was a frog in my drink,' cried Sennedjem. 'That boy...'

Horemheb looked angrily at me. He opened his mouth, but Ay put a hand on his arm.

'Horemheb, he's the pharaoh's friend. And he's young. Once, you were young, too.'

Ay looked at us and smiled.

He was often friendly like this, and helped us – but when I looked at him, I thought of a snake. Why did I think of a snake? Was it his small eyes? Was it his body? Was it his teeth? I did not know. Was he a good man? Perhaps. Perhaps not.

Horemheb looked angrily at me.

The Festival of Opet

E very year in Egypt, there was an important festival called Opet. Opet was a festival for the god Amun, and it was important for the Egyptians, because they wanted Amun to be happy. When he was happy, they thought, he could help them.

Amun's statue was in Karnak, a temple to the north of Thebes. For the festival, the Egyptian priests put the statue of Amun in a boat at Karnak, and then took it to the temple at Luxor with the pharaoh.

Statues of Amun's wife, Mut, and his son, Khons, came to Luxor in boats, too, and then more than thirty priests carried the statues into the temple. The people could watch from the river, but only Tutankhamun and some of the priests could go into the temple. The statues stayed in the temple for about twenty-four days. Then, when Amun's statue came out and went back to Karnak, the festival stopped.

One year, when we were about sixteen years old, I went with Tutankhamun to Karnak. We arrived there late at night, and early the next morning, when Tutankhamun was in the temple, I went to the river. His boat was there. It was beautiful. It was about thirty metres long and it had lots of gold on it.

There was an important festival called Opet.

I thought about my friend and felt sorry for him. 'His leg is hurting more and more,' I thought. 'And today is going to be a long day because he is taking the statue of Amun from Karnak to Luxor Temple.'

Then I thought of something. I looked for some nice, long reeds and took my knife from my pocket. I wanted to make something for my friend, but I needed to be quick. 'I don't have much time,' I thought. 'When Tutankhamun comes out of the temple, it must be ready.'

An hour or two later, I heard a noise and looked up. There they were – Tutankhamun and all the priests, with the statue of the god Amun. They came out of the temple and down to the river.

I stood up and ran to Tutankhamun with the thing in my hand.

'What is it?' Tutankhamun asked.

'A walking stick. I made it for you.'

Tutankhamun took the walking stick and looked at it happily. 'How did you make it?' he asked me.

'With reeds,' I said.

I heard chariots then, and Horemheb arrived. There were many soldiers in chariots behind him.

'Look!' said Tutankhamun to Horemheb. 'Aziru made this for me.'

Horemheb looked down at me. 'You made it?' he asked.

'Yes,' I said.

Horemheb smiled. 'Good boy,' he said.

Good boy! I wanted to laugh.

After that, everybody got on boats; and soon, they were ready. I could not go on Tutankhamun's gold boat – I was not the pharaoh – so I went on a smaller boat behind. Slowly at first, but then more quickly, all the boats moved away from Karnak.

Then I saw Tutankhamun. He stood up and called to me, and he had the new walking stick in his hand.

'Good boy!' he cried, and he looked down at me like Horemheb.

I laughed for a long time after that.

Tutankhamun had the new walking stick in his hand.

IIII
III
The Call of the Jackal

Tutankhamun was always tired after the Festival of Opet. So when the festival finished, he often went to his palace in Memphis, in the north of Egypt. From Memphis, Tutankhamun could easily visit Giza.

There were three big pyramids at Giza: the pyramid of Khafre, the pyramid of Khufu, and the pyramid of Menkaure. Menkaure was the smallest of these, but it was taller than the tallest temple in Egypt. Many years before, when pharaohs died, the Egyptians put their bodies into pyramids. But now, pharaohs had their tombs in the Valley of the Kings.

There were three big pyramids at Giza.

The pyramids were interesting, and Tutankhamun liked to see them – but he liked to go out and look for animals in the hills there more!

One year, when we were about eighteen, we left Memphis for Giza later than usual. It was afternoon when we came down to the river, and Tutankhamun's boat was ready. Near the boat, there were many soldiers in chariots. Tutankhamun got into his boat, and we suddenly heard a cry.

'Don't go!' called Ay. 'Wait, please! Wait!'

We looked up and saw Ay with Ankhesenamun, Tutankhamun's wife. Because Ay was an old man, he could not walk quickly, so we waited.

'What is Ay's man carrying?' asked Tutankhamun.

'I don't know,' I said. 'Let's wait and see.'

'What's the matter?' Tutankhamun asked when Ay arrived at the boat.

'This is for you,' said Ay, and he gave Tutankhamun a shield. There was a picture of Tutankhamun and lions on it. 'My workers finished it minutes ago.'

'Thank you, Ay,' said Tutankhamun, and he looked carefully at the shield. 'It's beautiful.'

Ay smiled again and his small eyes moved quickly. 'Good luck in Giza, my pharaoh,' he said. 'Please be careful.'

'I always am,' said Tutankhamun.

'That's not true!' his wife laughed.

There was a picture of Tutankhamun and lions on the shield.

Tutankhamun smiled, and the boat began to move away down the river.

We arrived in Giza two hours later, and it was night when we went out into the hills. There were soldiers with us, but Tutankhamun was the pharaoh, so he was in front. We walked slowly and stopped. We listened. There was no noise; nothing moved. We began walking again and suddenly I saw something at my feet.

Footprints.

I looked at them carefully: I did not want to be wrong. And I was not. 'Over here,' I called quietly.

Horemheb ran quickly to me, and Tutankhamun came behind, with his walking stick.

'What is it?' asked Horemheb, but then he saw the footprints, too. He looked at them carefully. Then, after a minute, he spoke. 'Yes,' he said. 'These are a lion's.'

'But the lion can't walk well, I think,' said Tutankhamun. 'These footprints don't look right.'

'We're close to it,' said Horemheb. 'When we find it, you can kill it.'

Then we heard a great roar: the noise of the lion, not far from us.

'Come!' said Horemheb. 'Quickly!'

We went up the hill and then we saw it: a beautiful, orange-gold lion.

For a second, it did not see Tutankhamun or our men; then suddenly its eyes were on us.

'Kill it, Pharaoh!' cried Horemheb, 'Now!'

But Tutankhamun did not. 'Look at its leg,' he said. 'It has a bad leg. I cannot kill it.'

There were more soldiers near us now, and Tutankhamun called to them. 'Don't kill it,' he said.

The soldiers stopped. The lion looked at the soldiers; then it opened its mouth and gave a great roar. When it was quiet again, it looked at Tutankhamun. Then, slowly, it walked away into the night.

'Don't kill it,' Tutankhamun said.

When we arrived back at the palace in Memphis that night, we were not tired, and Tutankhamun wanted to play senet, an Egyptian game. Tutankhamun was a good player, and I was, too. It was a warm night, and we played for two hours or more.

We played senet for two hours or more.

In our last game, Tutankhamun went onto the House of Water. I needed a three, and I got it and finished the game. I was happy. Tutankhamun smiled, took his walking stick, and stood up. But then something happened.

'What was that?' he asked.

'What?' I said.

'I heard a jackal,' said Tutankhamun, and he looked at the dark hills. 'Listen! There it is again.'

But I could not hear a jackal.

I looked at Tutankhamun and he looked at me. We said nothing more, but I felt afraid. The god Anubis, one of the gods of the dead, was a jackal. Why did Tutankhamun hear it when I did not?

We said goodnight and went to our rooms. But that night, I had a bad dream.

My dream began in a temple in Thebes. There, priests carried a dead ostrich to a table and put flowers on it. After that, Ankhesenamun came into the temple. When she saw the dead bird, she cried – she could not stop. Then my dream changed. I was on a boat. The boat went from east to west across the Nile to the Valley of the Kings. The ostrich was in the boat, but now it was gold. I could hear a name.

And the name was 'Tutankhamun'.

||||
||||

The Ostrich Fan

Early the next morning, when I opened my eyes, I thought about my dream and the game of senet the night before. I felt very tired, and I wanted to sleep, but I heard the noise of soldiers and chariots, and then Tutankhamun came into my room.

'Aziru!' he said. 'How are you?'

'I'm alive,' I said.

Tutankhamun laughed. 'I can see that!'

I smiled up at Tutankhamun. He looked different today.

'Are you going out in your chariot?' I asked.

'Yes,' he said. 'Horemheb and I are going north.'

'North? But why...?' I began to ask, but stopped.

One of Tutankhamun's men was there in the room with us. I sat up and looked at the man. He moved a fan slowly up and down over Tutankhamun's head. Everybody needed fans on hot days. But on this fan, there was a picture...

'No!' I cried.

'What's the matter?' asked Tutankhamun.

'There's a gold ostrich on the fan!' I said.

'Yes, there is. But I don't understand – what's wrong with that?' said Tutankhamun.

'I saw it in my dream last night. Something bad is

going to happen. Don't go out in your chariot today. Stay in the palace! Please listen to me.'

'But I can't stay. My men are working on one of Amun's temples, and I need to go and look at it. You wait here and sleep.'

'No,' I said again, but Tutankhamun walked to the door.

'Wait,' I called, but he did not stop. He walked away. The man with the fan left, too; and the room went quiet.

'There's a gold ostrich on the fan!'

Later that day, Tutankhamun's men brought him back to the palace.

'What happened?' I asked when I saw him.

'It was an accident,' said Horemheb. 'He was in his chariot and then it hit something. He broke his leg.'

Was it really an accident, I thought? Many people wanted to be the new pharaoh – did one of them hurt him?

Some soldiers took Tutankhamun to his room, and Ankhesenamun stayed with him all night. The next morning, he was a little better. But then the fever came. Ay brought a doctor – the best doctor in Egypt, he said – but Tutankhamun's fever did not stop. Soon, Tutankhamun was very ill. He stopped talking, and he did not know me, Ankhesenamun, Horemheb, or Ay.

Not long after, Tutankhamun, my friend, died. Many people in Egypt thought, 'Someone killed Tutankhamun for his crown.'

My best friend was dead, and for many days I did not leave the palace. I did not want to see people; I wanted to cry for Tutankhamun, the boy-king.

The priests took his body to the temple at Thebes. Then, after more than seventy days, they took him to the Valley of the Kings. His tomb was not ready, so they put him in a smaller one. After that, the priests read from the Book of the Dead and opened his mouth. They did this because Tutankhamun needed to eat and drink in the afterlife.

Later, the priests brought many things: his chair, his crook and flail, his crown, his walking sticks, his shield, his senet game – and the fan. He needed these in the afterlife, too.

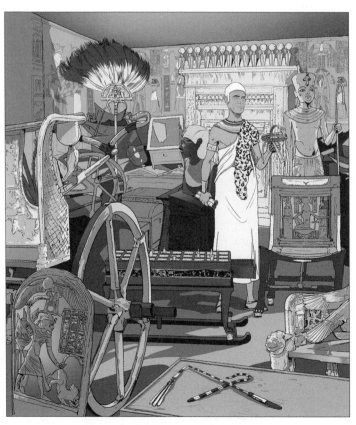

The priests brought many things.

Then they closed the door of the tomb...

And there, Anubis, the god of the dead, came to meet him. There was more good than bad in Tutankhamun, Anubis said, so he could go and live in the afterlife and be happy there for all time.

But in Egypt, some people were more interested in the pharaoh's crown.

'I am from the pharaoh's family,' Ay said. 'Listen to the gods. "Ay is the next pharaoh," they say.'

The priests liked Ay, so soon he wore the pharaoh's crown. But not for long. After three years, he died, and Horemheb was the next Egyptian pharaoh.

In the end, I left the palace, but I did not go back to Amurru: my father was dead, and the Hittites were there. I stayed in Egypt and found a wife: a beautiful Egyptian woman. I was happy and rich.

But I never forgot my friend, Pharaoh Tutankhamun. I am an old man now, and I have white hair and a walking stick, too. I love living in Egypt with my family, but I want to see my friend again.

Perhaps he is waiting in the afterlife for me.

Inside Tutankhamun's Tomb

Three thousand years after Tutankhamun died, Howard Carter, an Englishman, came to the Valley of the Kings. Carter knew about Tutankhamun, and he wanted to find his tomb. His friend, Lord Carnarvon, wanted to find it, too. Lord Carnarvon gave Carter some money and went back to England, and Carter began looking. But for the next five years, he found nothing.

In 1922, Lord Carnarvon spoke to Carter. 'You must stop working,' he said. 'There is no lost tomb in the Valley of the Kings. I cannot give you more money.'

'No!' said Carter. 'We can't stop now. Let's look for one more year. Please!'

'All right,' said Lord Carnarvon. 'But only for one more year.'

Carter went back to the Valley of the Kings. He worked and worked, but he found nothing. Then, on 4 November 1922, his men saw a door under the tomb of Pharaoh Rameses VI. There was a name on the door. And the name was 'Tutankhamun'.

Lord Carnarvon came to Egypt at once, and he and Carter opened the door. There was nothing behind that door, but they found a second door, and Carter looked through it.

*Howard Carter and Lord Carnarvon
at Tutankhamun's tomb, 1922*

'What can you see?' asked Lord Carnarvon.

For a minute, Carter could not speak. Then he said, 'Wonderful things!'

There was a room behind the door, and in the room were gold chairs, tables, chariots, and two big statues of Tutankhamun.

When the men broke down the door and went into the room, they found a third door next to the statues. In the room behind that door, they saw a beautiful coffin, in a big box. In the coffin, there was a second coffin, and then a third, gold one. When Carter opened the third coffin, he found Tutankhamun's body. There was a mask on his head, and it was blue and gold, and had a vulture and a snake on it.

When people heard about the tomb, they wanted to see Tutankhamun's beautiful things. Suddenly, everybody knew the name of the boy-king. Carter and his men worked for years in the tomb. They wrote about it and took photos, and then, very carefully, took everything to Egypt's biggest city, Cairo.

Many of the things are there today, and every year, more than a million people go and look at them. They see Tutankhamun's beautiful old chair, and the pharaoh's crook and flail and crown. They see his walking stick, his senet game, and a shield with pictures of lions. And they see a fan, too - a fan with an ostrich on it.

Tutankhamun's coffin and body.

GLOSSARY

boat *(n)* a small ship

chariot *(n)* a vehicle like a very small car, from ancient times; a horse or horses pulled it

city *(n)* a big and important town

coffin *(n)* a box for a dead body

crown *(n)* a gold circle with beautiful stones (called jewels); a king or queen wears it on his/her head

cup *(n)* You drink e.g. coffee from a cup.

dream *(n)* a picture in your head when you are sleeping

fall *(v)* to go down suddenly (past tense **fell**)

fan *(n)* A fan can move the air when you are hot.

festival *(n)* a special time when people have fun, dance, make music, etc.

fever *(n)* When you have a fever, your body is very hot because you are ill.

field *(n)* a piece of land for animals or for growing food, usually with a fence, trees, etc. around it

footprint *(n)* a picture on the ground from your foot or shoe

game *(n)* something you play that has rules

god *(n)* Religious people believe in a god, or gods, that they cannot see.

gold *(n & adj)* an expensive yellow metal

great *(adj)* very, very good, or big

grow *(v)* to become bigger (past tense **grew**)

hieroglyphics *(n)* ancient Egyptian writing, with pictures

hurt *(v)* to feel pain (when a part of your body feels bad); to do bad things to people (past tense **hurt**)

king *(n)* the most important man in a country

life *(n)* a person's time of being alive

mask *(n)* You wear a mask on your face; it hides or protects you.

palace *(n)* a very large house for a king or queen

papyrus *(n)* paper for writing and drawing in ancient Egyptian times (plural **papyri**)

plague *(n)* a disease or illness; it moves quickly from person to person, and kills many

powerful *(adj)* very strong and important

priest *(n)* an important religious person

pyramid *(n)* a big building with three or four sides or faces; the sides come together in a point at the top

reed *(n)* a tall plant, like grass; it grows in or near water

shield *(n)* a big piece of metal, wood, etc.; soldiers carried shields in front of their bodies

small *(adj)* not big; little

soldier *(n)* a person in an army; he/she fights for his/her country

star *(n)* a small bright light in the sky at night

statue *(n)* a stone or metal model of a person or animal

stick *(n)* a long piece of wood

temple *(n)* a religious building; people pray to their god or gods here

tomb *(n)* a place made of stone for a dead person's body

valley *(n)* the low land between mountains; there is often a river in it

ANIMALS IN THIS STORY

vulture

jackal

ostrich

snake

STORY NOTES

afterlife Egyptians believed in a new life after this one, called the afterlife. In their afterlife, people needed many of the things from their old life, so Egyptians put chairs, tables, games, food, etc. in a dead person's tomb with them.

Akhenaten pharaoh of Egypt from 1352–1336 BCE

Amun one of the most powerful gods in Ancient Egypt; in pictures, he often had two ostrich feathers on his head

Amurru an old country, where Syria and Lebanon are today

Anubis the god of the dead; he had the head of a jackal, and took people into the afterlife

Aten the Sun God

Isis the goddess of many things, e.g. children, mothers, and love; in Egyptian stories, the Nile flooded every year when Isis cried for her dead husband

Rameses VI pharaoh of Egypt from 1145–1137 BCE

senet An Egyptian game; the game had thirty squares, and players moved their pieces from square to square. Some of the squares were good for the players, but when they moved onto the square called the House of Water, they lost their go, and their piece.

Smenkhkare pharaoh of Egypt from 1335–1334 BCE

ABOUT ANCIENT EGYPT

Thousands of years ago, people came and lived near the River Nile, in north-east Africa. The river was good for them: they got water from it, went up and down it by boat, and could easily grow food for their families and their animals. They made towns and villages, and their kings and queens ruled over them – they told the people what they could and could not do. These people were the ancient Egyptians, and they lived like this for more than 3,000 years, from about 3100 BCE.

How the Egyptians lived

Most Egyptians worked in the fields every day, but some did other jobs, bread-making and boat-building. People traded: they gave food or animals for other things, and all day, boats went up and down the Nile.

Egyptian people loved their families, and children were very important to them. Most children worked in the fields from when they were very young. But in their free time, they liked to play ball games, run, and swim in the river. Only the boys of rich Egyptians went to school.

We learned a lot from the Egyptians. They understood a lot about the body, and they could make paper from reeds. They gave us our 365-day year, too.

Gods and pharaohs

The Egyptians had hundreds of gods and goddesses, for many different things: some brought the flood every year, some helped the dead, and some were for towns and animals. In pictures, many of the gods were half-animals, or wore animal masks. The gods were important in Egypt, so people made many beautiful temples for them, and there were important festivals, too.

The pharaoh was the most powerful person in Egypt. Everything in Egypt was the pharaoh's, and everyone had to listen to him or her. Thirty different families of pharaohs ruled the country during Ancient Egyptian times.

How we know about the Egyptians

We know a lot about the Egyptians because they had writers called scribes, and the scribes wrote about important times. When there was fighting with soldiers from other countries, a festival, or the opening of a new temple, the scribes wrote about it.

The beautiful pictures from these times tell us about life in Egypt, too. There were often pictures on the walls of people's tombs, of all the good things in that person's life. The things were in the picture because the person wanted to take them into the afterlife.

The Boy-King Tutankhamun

ACTIVITIES

ACTIVITIES

Before Reading

1 Match the <u>underlined</u> words in the sentences to the meanings below.

1 I love that <u>music</u>.

2 The <u>palace</u> has 54 rooms.

3 Tutankhamun's <u>tomb</u> was in the Valley of the Kings.

4 She's a very <u>powerful</u> woman.

5 Three million people live in this <u>city</u>.

a a place for a dead body

b a big and important town

c singing or playing instruments

d strong and important

e where a king / queen lives

2 Look at the front and back covers. Are these sentences true or false?

1 Tutankhamun was an Egyptian pharaoh.

2 He was a pharaoh when he was only a boy.

3 He died 5,000 years ago.

4 A man called Howard Carter found his tomb.

5 In the story, Tutankhamun and Aziru are brothers.

6 Tutankhamun is very famous today.

ACTIVITIES

While Reading

Read Chapter 1. Answer the questions.

1 Where is the Valley of the Kings?
2 What is the Egyptian name for the Valley of the Kings?
3 Today, what do many people take to the Valley of the Kings?
4 How many Egyptian pharaohs are there in the valley?
5 When did people find Tutankhamun's tomb?

Read Chapter 2. Match the people to the descriptions.

1 the Hittites	a son of the king of Amurru
2 Akhenaten	b Akhenaten's youngest son
3 Aziru	c Akhenaten's oldest son
4 Tutankhaten	d people from north of Amurru
5 Smenkhkare	e the pharaoh of Egypt

Read Chapter 3. Complete the sentences with names.

1 When _____ died, the priests took his body to a tomb near Amarna.
2 The people sang for their new pharaoh, _____.
3 Aziru was friends with a green parakeet called

_____.

4 _____ always liked to sit in his father's old chair.
5 _____ was angry when the parakeet called out.

Read Chapter 4. Put the events in order.

a The pharaoh's palace moved to Thebes.

b Akhenaten stopped the people having lots of gods.

c Tutankhaten began to wear the pharaoh's crown.

d The pharaoh built new temples for the old gods, and the people were happy again.

e Tutankhaten changed his name.

f Smenkhkare died.

Are these sentences true or false?

1 The people were angry because they only had one god and he could not stop the plague.

2 Ay and Horemheb wanted to move to Thebes.

3 Aziru drew Tutankhamun in his pharaoh's crown.

4 Aziru didn't want to move to Thebes.

Read Chapter 5. Circle the correct words in each sentence.

1 Tutankhamun had a wife called *Sennedjem / Ankhesenamun.*

2 Before a flood, Egyptians often saw *Sothis / Isis.*

3 *Tutankhamun / Aziru* was a good student.

4 Aziru put a *snake / frog* in his teacher's drink.

Who do you think likes Aziru? Write *Yes* or *No*.

1 Tutankhamun
2 Sennedjem
3 Horemheb

Read Chapter 6. Correct the <u>underlined</u> words to make true sentences.

1 The Opet festival in Egypt was for the god <u>Aten</u>.
2 The priests and the pharaoh took the god's statue to the temple at <u>Karnak</u>.
3 The statues stayed in the temple for <u>thirty</u> days.
4 Aziru made a walking stick for <u>Amun</u>.
5 Horemheb and his soldiers arrived in <u>boats</u>.

Read Chapter 7. Match the two parts of the sentences.

1 Tutankhamun liked visiting Giza because he…
2 Ay arrived at the boat late because his…
3 The lion's footprints did not look right because it…
4 Tutankhamun and Aziru played senet because they…
5 Aziru was afraid because Tutankhamun…

a had a bad leg.
b were not tired.
c gold workers made a shield for Tutankhamun.
d heard a jackal.
e liked looking for animals in the hills.

Read Chapter 8. Complete the sentences.

1 Tutankhamun wanted to go out in his c_____.

2 Aziru was afraid because there was an o_____ on the fan.

3 Tutankhamun was very ill; he had a f_____.

4 The priests put Tutankhamun's body into a small t_____.

5 After Anubis came to see him, Tutankhamun went to live in the a_____.

Read the sentences and write *Yes*, *No*, or *Don't know*.

1 Tutankhamun died because he broke his leg.

2 The priests put Tutankhamun's crook and flail in his tomb.

3 Ay wanted to be the next pharaoh.

4 Aziru went back to his father's country.

Read Chapter 9. What did Howard Carter find in the Valley of the Kings?

1 a door with the name 'Tutankhamun'

2 statues of Tutankhamun

3 Tutankhamun's coffins

4 Nefer the parakeet

5 the statue of Amun from the Karnak temple

6 a shield with pictures of lions

ACTIVITIES

After Reading

Vocabulary

1 Unscramble the words to complete the sentences.

1 Egyptians took their pharaohs' bodies to the
_____ (alVyle) of the Dead.

2 The _____ (agulpe) killed many people in Egypt.

3 When Tutankhamun went to Giza, Ay gave him a
_____ (dishle).

4 In Aziru's _____ (marde), there was a dead
ostrich.

5 In his coffin, Tutankhamun wore a blue and gold
_____ (skam).

2 Look at the words below. Write *Person, Animal, Thing,* or *Place.*

1 king	9 field	
2 city	10 cup	
3 bird	11 palace	
4 boat	12 pharaoh	
5 soldier	13 frog	
6 jackal	14 coffin	
7 chariot	15 priest	
8 snake	16 temple	

Grammar

1 **Choose the correct words to complete the sentences.**

The Egyptians put the bodies of their dead pharaohs
(*into*)/ *above* beautiful coffins.

1 Akhenaten's tomb was *next to* / *near* Amarna.

2 In his picture, Aziru wore a crown *on* / *onto* his head.

3 In the school room, Aziru sat *next to* / *under*
Tutankhamun.

4 Sennedjem took a big drink *in* / *from* his cup.

5 A fan moved slowly up and down *over* / *on*
Tutankhamun's head.

2 **Complete the sentences using the past simple tense of the
words below.**

come   find   give   make   put   ~~sing~~   think

Aziru _____*sang*_____ because Egypt had a new pharaoh.

1 Aziru _____ to Egypt from Amurru.

2 Aziru _____ a walking stick for Tutankhamun.

3 In Memphis, Ay _____ a shield to Tutankhamun.

4 In the morning, Aziru _____ about his dream.

5 The priests _____ many things in Tutankhamun's
tomb.

6 Carter's men _____ a door under Rameses VI's
tomb.

Reading

1 Find the words on the pages below. Who/What are they talking about?

page 4 – them – *the Hittites*

1 page 6 – him
2 page 17 – it
3 page 20 – me
4 page 26 – these
5 page 29 – you
6 page 33 – us

2 Correct the <u>underlined</u> word in each sentence to make the story true.

When he was <u>nine</u> years old, Aziru left Amurru. He went to the pharaoh's palace in <u>Thebes</u>, in Egypt. At first, Aziru's only friend was a green <u>frog</u>. But soon he was great friends with Tutankhaten, Pharaoh Smenkhkare's <u>son</u>. Smenkhkare died when Tutankhaten was <u>seven</u>, so then he was pharaoh. He wanted to please the god <u>Aten</u>, so he took the name Tutankhamun. He moved to <u>Amarna</u>, too. He built new palaces, and the people loved him.

One day, Aziru had a bad dream about <u>a jackal</u>. The next day, Tutankhamun was in a <u>boat</u> accident. When he died, the priests put his body in a tomb in <u>Giza</u>. In <u>1923</u>, Howard Carter opened it and found wonderful things.

Writing

1 Look at the picture on page 10 and complete the description.

This picture is from Chapter _____. In the picture,
we can see Tutankhaten, Horemheb, Aziru, and the parakeet
called _____. _____ is afraid, and Horemheb
is looking at the parakeet. Tutankhaten is standing next
to a _____. He is smiling because the parakeet is
saying 'Horemheb is _____!' In the story, after this,
Horemheb walks away, and Tutankhaten and Aziru can't
stop _____.

2 Look at the picture on page 34 and answer the questions.

1 Which chapter is this picture in?
2 Who and what can we see in the picture?
3 What are they doing?
4 What happens in the story after this?

3 Use your answers to write a description of the picture.

4 Choose another picture from the story and write a description.

Speaking

1 Read the words below. Replace the words in bold to make the sentences true.

Cairo   doctor   Horemheb
smaller   Tutankhaten   worse

1 **Smenkhkare** was Akhenaten's youngest son.
2 **Thebes** is the biggest city in Egypt.
3 The crook was **bigger** than the flail.
4 **Ay** was the most powerful soldier in Egypt.
5 Aziru was a **better** student than Tutankhamun.
6 Ay brought Tutankhamun the best **priest** in Egypt.

2 Underline the language in exercise 1 used to compare.

3 Discuss the questions with a partner.

1 Who was most important in Tutankhamun's life?
2 Who was more powerful, Tutankhamun or Ay?
3 Who was Aziru more afraid of, Horemheb or Ay?

4 Complete these sentences with your own words. Say them to a partner. Does he/she agree? Why/Why not?

1 … was the funniest part of the story.
2 Chapter … was the best chapter.
3 The most interesting thing I learned was …
4 The best character in the story was …
5 This book was better than …

THE OXFORD BOOKWORMS LIBRARY

THE OXFORD BOOKWORMS LIBRARY is a best-selling series of graded readers which provides authentic and enjoyable reading in English. It includes a wide range of original and adapted texts: classic and modern fiction, non-fiction, and plays. There are more than 250 Bookworms to choose from, in seven carefully graded language stages that go from beginner to advanced level.

Each Bookworm is illustrated, and offers extensive support, including:

▸ a glossary of above-level words
▸ activities to develop language and communication skills
▸ notes about the author and story
▸ online tests

Each Bookworm pack contains a reader and audio.

|6| **STAGE 6** ▸ 2500 HEADWORDS ▸ CEFR B2–C1
|5| **STAGE 5** ▸ 1800 HEADWORDS ▸ CEFR B2
|4| **STAGE 4** ▸ 1400 HEADWORDS ▸ CEFR B1–B2
|3| **STAGE 3** ▸ 1000 HEADWORDS ▸ CEFR B1
|2| **STAGE 2** ▸ 700 HEADWORDS ▸ CEFR A2–B1
|1| **STAGE 1** ▸ 400 HEADWORDS ▸ CEFR A1–A2
|S| **STARTER** ▸ 250 HEADWORDS ▸ CEFR A1

Find a full list of *Bookworms* and resources at
www.oup.com/elt/gradedreaders

If you liked this Bookworm, why not try...

47 Ronin: A Samurai Story from Japan
JENNIFER BASSETT

When Lord Asano drew his sword on Lord Kira one spring day in 1701, it began a story that is now a national legend in Japan.